BRENDA PAGE

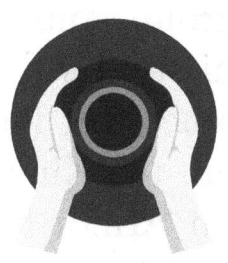

SHAPED FOR PURPOSE

IN THE HANDS OF THE POTTER

© Copyright 2020 by Brenda Page

All rights reserved. This book is protected under the copyright laws of the United States of America. This book may not be copied or reprinted for commercial gain or profit. The use of short quotations or an occasional page copied for personal or group study is permitted and encouraged. Permission will be granted upon request. Unless otherwise identified, Scripture quotations are from the King James Version of the Bible. The poem "Armor-bearer," may be used by permission of Bridget Williams.

Take note that the name satan and related names are not capitalized. We choose not to acknowledge him, even to the point of violating grammatical rules.

ISBN: 978-0-9679441-6-6

Published By
All That Productions, Inc.
P.O. Box 1594
Humble, Texas 77347-1594

Dedication

This book is dedicated to the loving memory of my grandmother, Luberta Gillespie.

Acknowledgments

To my Father in heaven, to Him be all the glory, honor and praise for the great and wonderful work that He has done in my life.

To my daughter, Erica Page Warner, who is my blessing from God. To my godchildren with whom God has so richly blessed me: Frear twins, Kimberly Mack, Cecelia, Biancia, Dominique, and Freniscia.

To Timothy McCray, I thank you for your English ability that got me started. To Momma, Annette, and Sister Resha. Thank you for proofreading and making changes in my manuscript. Thank you so much.

To Nerissa, thanks so much for every encouraging word. To Yolonda, thanks a million for the many hours and days that you spent typing, Deborah Elum, for your publishing ability, and Minister Frank, for helping with the cover.

To Queen and Mellonie, thank you so much for all of your prayers and wisdom and my prayer partner, Coliss Arabb, for every prayer and every connection.

To my Universal Church family and missionary sisters, thanks a million for encouraging me and praying for me. To all the saints, my friends, and family whom I might not have called by name, thank you. For if our lives had not crossed, then I would not have been able to share what life and experience has taught me.

Foreword

Thanks be to God who has blessed me to be the proud Pastor of this daughter in the Lord. What a blessing to the work of soulwinning. It is encouragement to the heart of any servant of the Lord, when any of those that were snatched out of the devil's clutches, grow to use the things that were meant to destroy them, to deliver such a blow to the enemy.

Missionary Brenda Page is a member in good standing with the Universal Church of God in Christ, for whom I serve as Pastor. Sister Page has worked faithfully and has served as Deaconess, Youth President, Church Correspondence, Department President and is currently serving as chief adjutant to the First Lady, Evangelist Debra Hubbard.

She has grown in the challenges that come to all who live, love, and work for the Lord. God has and is showing us that life's disappointments can become testimonies to Him. It is a blessing to all of us when any of us is able to make an impact for God in any way. What an uplifting and refreshing joy to know that we are more than conquerors in Christ Jesus. May God ever bless you.

- Pastor Freddie Hubbard Sr.

Table of Contents

Introduction: In the Hands of the Potter 13

Chapter 1 | The Call of God 19

Chapter 2 | Chosen 25

Chapter 3 | Anointed 35

Summary 43

Tribute to My Mentor 47

Endorsements 49

About the Author 51

Words from the Potter 53

Surely your turning of things upside down shall be esteemed as the Potter's clay: For shall the work say of him that made it, He made me not? or shall the thing framed say of him that framed it, He had no understanding?

Isaiah 29:16

INTRODUCTION

In the Hands of the Potter

For I know the thoughts that I think toward you, saith the LORD, thoughts of peace, and not of evil, to give you an expected end.

Jeremiah 29:11

Growing up as a child, so many things transpired that caused me to wonder if any thing good would come out of my life. I was raised in a dysfunctional family, and had dreams of being used by God which seemed to be only that, a dream.

INTRODUCTION: IN THE HANDS OF THE POTTER

I remember playing in our backyard with my brother Billy, and friend, Kathy. We loved to play church. We would sing and jump around pretending to shout. Then, I would preach and teach the Word.

I really didn't understand why the enemy was trying so hard to destroy me, to take away the plan and purpose God had for my life. But thanks be to God because He kept me alive and brought me into His kingdom for such a time as this. I have learned that when we surrender our lives totally and commit our ways to God, we set ourselves up to be used by Him.

The hand of the Lord worked a mighty miracle when He allowed me to move in with my grandmother, Luberta Gillespie. She was a Missionary and great woman of God. She taught and trained me from an early age about the importance of discipline and the Word of God.

> [12] So after he (Jesus) had washed their feet, and had taken his garments, and was set down again, he said unto them, Know ye what I have done to you?
> [13] Ye call me Master and Lord: and ye say well; for so I am.
> [14] If I then, your Lord and Master, have washed

your feet; ye also ought to wash one another's feet.

¹⁵ For I have given you an example, that ye should do as I have done to you.

¹⁶ Verily, verily, I say unto you, The servant is not greater than his lord; neither he that is sent greater than he that sent him.

John 13:12-16

Greatness Comes Through Serving Others

"You are only great when you can humble yourself and wait on God's people," my grandmother used to say. My grandmother would hold Missionary meetings at our house. They would come together to pray. I had to serve the sandwiches, the coffee, and to make sure all their needs were met.

After they would leave, I had to clean up. I used to tell my grandmother if serving and cleaning up is what the "Work of the Lord" is all about, then I pass. I wanted no part of being a servant. Of course, she would rebuke me and say there is no greater service than to serve the people of God. I had no idea that this training would lead me into the divine destiny for my life.

INTRODUCTION: IN THE HANDS OF THE POTTER

A Divine Encounter with Jesus

At the age of seven, the Lord Jesus himself visited me. In those wonderful minutes, my life took on a new purpose and a new meaning. I wanted to just stay in His presence and look upon the one I loved.

It was a beautiful fall evening, just before sunset. There I sat on the floor of the living room in front of the door with textbooks and homework papers scattered all about me. That was my favorite place for doing my homework. I loved to look outside at the beauty of nature, the beautiful brown, orange, and rust colored leaves on the trees.

As I gazed up to take a break from the paper, I saw something. It was large circle of light. The rays from the light reflected down and through the screen door. I could feel the warmth of the rays on my face. It was almost too bright to look at. The light was as bright as the noonday sun. As I closed my eyes and then opened them back up, I continued to feel this warmth that was so soothing and peaceful to me. I knew that this was not an ordinary experience. Then, I could see the image of a man in the circle; it was Jesus. He was very tall and His arms stretched out as far as my

INTRODUCTION: IN THE HANDS OF THE POTTER

eyes could see. The light was so awesome and bright; I could feel His love and peace all around me, as though I was wrapped in a blanket. I felt joy like I had never known before.

I began to feel as though something inside me was trying to get out. Then, tears began to run down my face. The tears were like rivers of water springing up out of my innermost being.

> [38] He that believeth on me, as the scripture hath said, out of his belly shall flow rivers of living water.
> [39] (But this spake he of the Spirit, which they that believe on him should receive: for the Holy Ghost was not yet given; because that Jesus was not yet glorified.)
>
> John 7:38-39

Before I knew it, my hands were up lifted and I knew that it was the beginning of something wonderful. My whole inside was shaking. I began to feel a tingling in my hands, then a surge went through my whole body. The more I tried to hold myself, the stronger the tingling and the shaking became. All I knew was that I didn't want anything to change, but then the light, the ray and the image began to fade away. The experience lasted for more than an hour.

INTRODUCTION: IN THE HANDS OF THE POTTER

Later on that night, I told my grandmother what had happened to me. As I knelt down in front of her, she told me that she already knew what was going on within me. God had already shown her what I would be. As she continued, she said, "As you began to grow, God himself would reveal it all to you."

She also told me that we can't run or hide from what God has ordained and chosen us to be before we were here. She told me that He is the one who directs and plans our lives if we listen to Him. Our lives are already laid; we just obey and follow. We are just vessels of clay in the hands of the Potter.

> [4] Then the word of the LORD came unto me, saying,
> [5] Before I formed thee in the belly I knew thee; and before thou camest forth out of the womb I sanctified thee, and I ordained thee a prophet unto the nations.
>
> Jeremiah 1:4-5

CHAPTER ONE

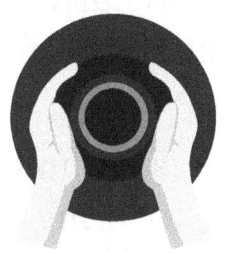

The Call of God

And I am convinced and sure of this very thing, that he who began a good work in you will continue until the day of Jesus Christ [right up to the time of his return], developing [that good work] and perfecting and bringing it to full completion in you.

Philippians 1:6 AMP

The call of God is only the beginning of the process. Only God knows the call He has on our lives. He wants to shape us so that we are ready

THE CALL OF GOD

to answer and step into our calling. We are first called to salvation. When we stay in His will we are able to give birth to purpose. Everyone should seek God as to what His perfect will is for his or her life.

The call of God is so unique in that it gives us an opportunity to bring God's purpose for our lives into full manifestation. Sometimes we struggle with the question "Am I called or not?" or "What am I called to do?" The call of God is very serious; it is not to be taken lightly.

> [For it is He] Who delivered and saved us and called us with a calling in itself holy and leading to holiness [to a life of consecration, a vocation of holiness]. He did it, not because of anything of merit that we have done, but because of and to further his own purpose and grace (unmerited favor) which was given us in Christ Jesus before the world began [eternal ages ago].
>
> 2 Timothy 1:9 AMP

Then, He calls us to be filled with the Holy Ghost to live holy and consecrated lives for Him. It's not only His call, but it's His will that we should live holy. Whether we are called to be an evangelist, pastor, teacher, or to any other ministries, the Scripture instructs us to make sure we are doing what God called us to do. In 2 Peter 1:10 it reads, *"Wherefore the rather, brethren, give diligence to make your calling and election sure: for if ye do these things, ye shall never fall."* He is the only one that can call us something on credit and help us arrive at the place that He called us to.

> Let every man abide in the same calling wherein he was called. Art thou called being a servant? Care not for it: but if thou mayest be made free, use it rather For he that is called in the Lord, being a servant, is the Lord's freeman likewise also he that is called, being free, is Christ's servant. Ye are bought with a price; be not ye the servants of men.
>
> 1 Corinthians 7:20-23

We have to understand that it is God that does the calling, the choosing, and the anointing for the work of church and the perfecting of the saints. Always remember, whatever office God calls you to do, He anoints you for that place. He is the one that does the work in our lives.

THE CALL OF GOD

So many times we are guilty of trying to make people be what we desire or want them to be. Sometimes we are so busy looking at what a person is or what he or she was, we can't see the hand of God in their lives. But thanks be to God, He see and knows what we shall be. We have to know that it is all in the Father's plan. The Scripture reads in Proverbs 19:21 (AMP), *"Many plans are in a man's mind, But it is the Lord purpose for him that will stand."*

Not only does God call but He also gives gifts to men. You can't work for them or merit them; they are gifts. Whatever God called you to do, He has gifted and qualified you for the job.

> Having the gifts differing according to the grace that is given to us whether prophecy, let us prophesy according to the proportion of faith: Or ministry, let us wait on our ministering: or he that teacheth, on teaching.
>
> Romans 12:6-7

We can never become so caught up in the gifts and calling that we forget about the Giver and the Creator of all things.

No Matter the Cost

We must be confident in knowing that God will come after everything in our lives, that will prevent His will from being done and His power working through us. The most important thing is to love God first. We have to be faithful, first to the one that called us and second, to the call. We have to stay dedicated to God no matter what comes into our lives. If we are truly called, we will remain, no matter what the cost may be. Up or down, live or die. We can stand because of our faith in the one that called us. We can and we will remain faithful to Him who has called us.

You have to stay before the Lord, seeking Him daily. The transformation in your live can only happen depending on how often you stay before God, allowing Him to restructure your vessel. It is so important that after you accept the call of God, you become teachable. You have to deposit the Word in you. Get in the Word and let the Word get into you. When God's Word is conceived in your heart and spoken out of your mouth, then you can walk in total victory.

Since I have applied the Word of God to my daily living, these principles have made me blessed. This has kept me focused, balanced, and sober. In Jeremiah 15:16 it says, *"Thy words were found, and I did eat them; and thy word was unto me the joy and rejoicing of mine heart: for I am called by thy name, O Lord God of hosts."*

When you truly love God and obey His Word you won't become intoxicated and drunk with the cares of this world. You have to stay on your face before God, fasting and praying to keep the intimacy forever flowing. Sit at the feet of Jesus Christ until He is formed in you.

> Blessed (happy, fortunate, prosperous, and enviable) is the man who walks and lives not in the counsel of the ungodly [following their advice, their plans and purpose], nor stands [submissive and inactive] in the path where sinners walk, nor sits down [to relax and rest] where the scornful [and the mockers] gather. But his delight and desire are in the Law of the Lord, and on His [the precepts, the instructions, the teachings of God]. He habitually meditates [ponders and studies] by Day and by Night.
>
> Psalm 1:1-2 AMP

CHAPTER TWO

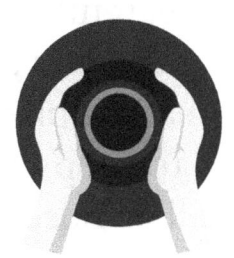

Chosen

> Ye have not chosen me, but I have chosen you, and ordained you, that ye should go and bring forth fruit, and that your fruit should remain: that what so ever ye shall ask of the Father in my name, he may give it you.
>
> John 15:16

The word chosen in the Hebrew language is the word "bachar." Bachar means to try, to examine, resulting in that which is tried, proven. God has chosen us, wonderfully shaped us, and destines us in accordance with His will.

The Lord chose me to minister as a Missionary. The ministry of the Word must have an important place in the life of the believer. As you minister to God, you have to be careful not to let the things of this world get between you and Him. You have to learn how to protect the place to which He has called you. You have to keep in mind that he who humbles himself shall be raised up.

After I served as a Missionary, God then called me into the Ministry of Helps as an armor-bearer. Since the moment the Holy Spirit revealed to me that I was an armor-bearer, I remembered when I served the missionaries in my grandmother's home. I remember serving my first pastor and his wife, Pastor Blaylock and Hazel. Then, I understood why I had so much joy serving others.

Pastor Blaylock and Sister Hazel, were very instrumental in my life. At the age of nine years old, I would help to clean up their house and the church. Hazel was a wonderful woman. I just loved to follow her around. Packing her shoes, Bible, and purse gave me the greatest of joy.

Pastor Blaylock could pray and make you feel as though the heavens had opened up. I will never forget the sermon that he preached that caused me to come to Jesus. He preached about Nicodemus and how you cannot enter the Kingdom of God without being born again. Even back then, there was something about God's Word that would make my insides leap. The preached Word of God brought such joy to my heart. I bless God for His undying love, for He chose me and bestowed His grace on my life. It was His good pleasure and His will to extend such an act of kindness.

Serving Others Abroad

Even as I child, I would dream of going abroad to minister to God's people. My desire and dream is one day go to Africa before the coming of the Lord.

I had a chance to travel to Jamaica and be a part of Reverend Jackie McCullough's Crusade. It was such an awesome experience, praying for the people, giving them medical and dental care, and making sure they had food to eat. That night under the tent, I shall never forget the praise and worship that went forth. They worship God like I had never seen before.

They seem to have so little, but love God so much. We have so much as Americans and we cheat God when it comes to our praises. Being there, seeing how people like Dr. Iona Locke and Minister Vickie Winans gave of themselves so freely; it was enough to inspire me to really do the will of God.

When I look back down through my life, I realized that waiting on and serving others has brought me joy and fulfillment. The Lord began to let me know that if I put my concerns in His hands, my work was not in vain. If I stayed focused on the vision of my Shepherd and the people of God, He would exalt me in due season.

An armor-bearer must have the heart of a servant. The basic job for an armor-bearer is, "to lift,to give help, to hold up, to respect, and to stir up." The poem Bridget Williams wrote for me describes the ministry of the armor-bearer.

Armor-Bearer
by
Bridget Williams

Brenda, get ready for Battle
Put the whole armor of God on
The Spirit World is getting ready to RATTLE!
The fighting has just begun!

CHOSEN

Put on the Helmet of Salvation,
to protect your Mind,
The Breastplate of Righteousness,
so no gaps can they find,
Gird your Loins about with Truth
Take hold the Shield of Faith and move forward
and take the Sword of the Spirit,
which is the Word of God!
Shod your feet
with the Preparation of the Gospel of Peace,
Pray fervently,
Pray and do not cease.
Bind the works of the enemy,
In the person's life
Bind every scheme,
envy, and strife
Pray for that person's strength
and will in the Lord
Pray always, Brenda and you will get
A Wonderful Reward!
Pray when you agree,
Pray when you don't
Pray in the midst of trouble,
Never say I won't

CHOSEN

Pray, pray it's the only way
To go higher in the Lord,
Please pray! Brenda pray.
The enemy will come after you,
as you cry out in their stead
Just keep the whole Armor of God on,
and don't be afraid,
Don't be manipulated,
Be Bold, Be Hard,
Stand on God's Word
and obey the voice of the Lord!
You are bearing the Arm for another
Someone who's in need,
"Speak Lord to their Heart
and they will follow your Lead."
Armor-bearer, Armor-bearer
Pray, Pray, Pray
Armor-bearer, Armor-bearer
Has no time to play
Armor-bearer, wear and bear the Armor well
Pray God's Word and you will never fail!

Don't Stay Where You Are

There is only one way to know the direction of God for your life. Continue to seek Him until He makes your calling sure. Take the story about Elisha in 1 Kings 19:19-20. He knew that his calling was to serve the prophet of God.

The prophet Elijah found Elisha, the son of Shapat, plowing in a field with twelve yoke of oxen before him, and he drove the twelfth: and Elijah passed by him, and cast his mantle upon him.

He left the oxen, and ran after Elijah, and said, "Let me, I pray thee, kiss my father and my mother, and then I will follow thee."

Elijah said unto him, "Go back again: for what have I done to thee?" He returned back from him, and took a yoke of oxen and slew them, and boiled their flesh with the instruments of the oxen, and gave unto the people, and they did eat. Then he arose, and went after Elijah, and ministered unto him. From the moment he met Elijah he was a transformed man.

The anointing in the life of Elijah awakens the destiny and purpose in Elisha's heart. He was willing to make a change to do what God had called him to do. Once he saw Elijah, he was ready to get up and move into the place where God's power was flowing. He was willing to step out and change direction. Because he changed, he eventually stepped into even a greater anointing as a great prophet of God, one who had double the anointing that was upon Elijah.

Just because you move into your calling it doesn't mean that it will be easy. You get tired, dirty, pushed aside, and sometimes even abused. Oh, but don't stop being faithful to the one that calls you. Never allow the flesh to stop you from moving into the plan of God for your life. Even in the face of adversity, you have to declare for God I live and for my God I will die.

> [7] But we have this treasure in earthen vessels, that the excellency of the power may be of God, and not of us.
> [8] We are troubled on every side, yet not distressed, we are perplexed, but not in despair;
> [9] Persecuted, but not forsaken; cast down, but not destroyed;
>
> 2 Corinthians 4:7-9

It is so important that we become "Spirit-controlled" and see things from God's perspective. We need to be rooted, grounded, and settled in the things of God. We have to be able to tell God that it's You that I love. We can't pray without You. We can't preach without You. We can't live without You!

To be effective in any calling, we must be willing and obedient in every area of our life. We don't control anything; we are vessels in the Master's hands. We must keep a heart of repentance and obedience in order for God to keep freedom in our lives as well to let the work of the Lord have free course in this hour. We might be living on the mountain but growth comes in the valley. Learn to go through no matter the cost.

> And Samuel said, Hath the Lord as great delight in burnt offerings and sacrifices, as in obeying the voice of the Lord? Behold, to obey is better than sacrifice, and to hearken than the fat of rams. For rebellion is as the sin of witchcraft, and stubbornness is as iniquity and idolatry, Because thou hast rejected the word of the Lord, he hath also rejected thee from being king.
>
> 1 Samuel 5:22-23

CHAPTER THREE

Anointed

The spirit of the Lord is upon me, because he hath anointed me to preach the gospel to the poor: he has sent me to heal the brokenhearted, to preach deliverance to the captives, and recovering of sight to the blind, to set at liberty them that are bruised. To preach the acceptable year of the Lord.

Luke 4:18-19

While pondering over this passage of Scripture, the Lord dropped a news flash on me. The same anointing gives me power over my life first. After the Gospel has been delivered to me, then I had the ability to lift someone else. It's His anointing that helps us fulfill everything that God has purposed us to do. Strong's Dictionary gives several Hebrew meanings for the word anointing; *Mashach* – to rub or smear with oil, to consecrate, and *Mashyach* – consecrated person such as a king, priest, or a saint.

There cannot be effective service without the anointing. The more you are consecrate, the more tests and trials you go through. It's a process in which God brings about a vessel of honor.

It's true that God does anoint you for the office to which He has called you. But for every level that God takes you to, there is a bigger devil. So, we are in need of a greater anointing to meet each challenge.

I remember when I first became an armor-bearer for Evangelist Hubbard. I had so many thoughts of how to be anointed as I followed her closely. She became the Elijah in my life. At that time, I really had not answered the call but I knew I had a desire to please the Lord. So I became Elisha. Not to take her place, but to be molded, shaped, and prepared for God's timing.

In order to have the power of God flowing through me, I had to become obedient to the will of God. During this period as I began to seek God more; I found out the increase of the anointing depended upon my obedience. I began to learn about God's ways and His will. He taught me that a real relationship is not just a casual thing.

Intimacy Brings Relationship

Out of your relationship with God, the anointing is birthed. If you want the power of God to become evident in your life, it begins with a true understanding of who He is. You have to commune with God in order to know His ways. It's not a one-night stand, it's a lifetime of commitment. It's a daily process of denial and surrendering your will to His will.

God is the source; Christ is the one that speaks the Word of God, and it's the Spirit of God that completes the process in our lives. I have found that in being anointed of God and seeking to bare His anointing, we cannot mix it with anything that is unholy. When we seek God's anointing, we have to become ready to be shaken and crushed and even beaten for His sake.

> Now he which stablisheth us with you in Christ, and hath anointed us in God: Who hath also sealed us, and gives the earnest of the Spirit in our hearts.
>
> 2 Corinthians 1:21-22

One very important thing you must keep ever before you is that all the glory and honor belongs to God. Never become guilty of robbing Him of His glory. Stay focused, clear and sober. Always remember what you are, He made you. What you have, He gave you. Anything that you ever hope to be is due to the love that He has for you. The love and mercy that He has for you causes Him to come to your aid.

> This I recall to my mind, therefore have I hope. It is of the Lord's mercies that we are not consumed, because his compassions fail not. They are new every morning: great is thy faithfulness.
>
> Lamentations 3:21-23

Even though God is faithful to you in bearing His anointing, God has to be able to trust you. This is no place for hidden agendas. When you mess up, always be ready and willing to repent. The price you pay to get the anointing is the price you pay to keep it.

To be effective in our calling, as well as our spiritual lives, we must continually go through a lifetime of process. Prayer has to be a priority in order to keep the newness in your ministry. Someone once said that when you pray often, you will seldom fail.

Baring God's anointing is so important to me. When I think about the great pioneers of the Gospel, it inspires me to keep the power of God flowing through my life.

It's high time we began to realize that it takes someone to lay their life down and impart spiritual truths in us so that we will be able to carry the vision and bring it's purpose into view. People like Smith Wigglesworth and Bishop Mason have always electrified my spirit to the point of wanting to keep the fire of the Holy Ghost and the passion for God alive today. I have even seen the spirit of Azusa living on in many ministries because of William J. Seymour.

I did not met Smith Wigglesworth, but I witnessed his legacy flowing down to Lester Sumrall. Now from Lester Sumrall to Rod Parsley.

I have seen that same anointing imparted in him. I have not met Kathryn Kuhlman but I met Benny Hinn in his crusades and witnessed the healing power of God that flowed through her now flows afresh through him.

I have come face to face with people like Elder Donnie McClurkin and have seen how the anointing is working in his life. I have been in the services and when he mounted the stage, I saw how his private worship met with his public worship and the atmosphere changed. No matter where you see him, he's the same all over the world.

I have never met Mother Coffney or Mother Boyd, but I have met Evangelist Debra Hubbard and I have embraced the anointing in her life because of them. I have walked with her and I have seen her cast the demonic spirits out of people. I have watched the anointing increase in her life. I have seen the sufferings in her life. If you want the anointing of God, you have to be willing to pay the price. The Word of God says, *"Mark the perfect man, and behold the upright: for the end of that man is peace" (Psalm 37:37).*

In seeing all that I have seen and all the places that I have traveled, I have experienced the real anointing for myself. You will never be able to flow in God's anointing until you become a servant of men. We must remember that God is a wonderful bookkeeper, so therefore no job will go unrewarded. So, I encourage you to walk in the anointing of God, submissive to the Father's divine will and authority, so that you will fulfill your ordained purpose.

Summary

My soul hath them still in remembrance, and is humbled in me. This I recall to my mind therefore I have hope. It is of the Lord's mercies that we are not consumed, because His compassions fail not. They are new every morning: great is thy faithfulness. The Lord is my portion: saith my soul: therefore will I hope in him, The Lord is good unto them that wait for him, to the soul that seeketh him.

Lamentations 3:20-25

I pray that this book will lift you to a place of prominence, challenge your walk with God, and give you courage to move into the perfect will of God. I pray that your heart will be encouraged and your faith will rise. I pray that in the content of these pages, you find the peace you need in your life. I pray that your purpose be revealed and that you know God in a very real way.

SUMMARY

It is also my heart-felt prayer that after reading this book, you will find healing in the Scriptures, stability in your walk, peace in your mind, and freedom in your life. I have learned that the gift of suffering brings us closer to God. For if we can let go of the pain, we will be healed. It's in forgiving that healing does come. When we come close to God, He transforms our life.

I thank God for His Spirit that has given me wisdom and revelation to know the hope in which I have been called. I pray for the saints everywhere that God will reveal His purpose in the lives of His people. I pray that He gives you purpose in your heart and mind, enabling you to arrive at a place of maturity in Him.

SUMMARY

Prayer

I pull down every stronghold in your life in the mighty name of Jesus and that you walk worthy of your calling. I pray that your walk lines up with the Word of God. I pray for abundance in your life and the anointing of God to flow freely through you. I pray for a fresh filling of the Holy Ghost and that the eyes of your understanding be opened. May the Lord keep you with a repentant heart and a humble spirit. May the peace of God dwell in your heart, your faith be lifted, and your walk be strengthened. I bless the Lord for His holiness and I praise Him for His faithfulness. I bless the Lord for His hand in the life of His people. May God continue to give joy, peace, and love in the Holy Ghost. Amen

- Missionary Brenda Page

Tribute To My Mentor

To my mentor, Evangelist Debra Hubbard, you have been such an inspiration in my life. For being an instrument in the Master's Hand, I am grateful. I would like to express my appreciation and my gratitude for you walking into a shipwrecked life and imparting so much of yourself to me. To God be the glory for His mercy and His faithfulness toward me. I came to you with hurts and wounds. You introduced me to the Healer. I came with walls and all locked in; you have shown me how to triumph. You taught me patience, discipline, and accountability.

I thank you for the times when you were in my face and confronted me. Not only did you tell me, but you also took me by the hand until I could clearly understand. When I couldn't walk, you carried me. When I was afraid of the past, you have shown me courage to see there is a future.

TRIBUTE TO MY MENTOR

You challenged me to rise up, when I wanted to fall. You taught me to laugh, when I wanted to cry; to persevere and to go through. To close my mouth and pray until something happens. Out of everything that you did, the most important thing you taught me is to know God in a very real way. It's called a relationship.

Love Always, Page
Your Armor-bearer

Endorsements

To my most dearest and longest friend. I've always knew that you would do something great with your life, but I thought it would be a restaurant, but I would have been proud of you whatever it was. So you just keep on keeping on until your number is called. Love you for the rest of my life, your soul mate sister.

Kathy E. Bailey

Friends are like angels who lift us to our feet, when our wings have trouble remembering how to fly. "Be Blessed."

Love Ya (Jesse) Sis. Alma McCray

ENDORSEMENTS

The Lord has truly blessed you with a gift of encouraging His people through your divinely inspired writings. I am so godly proud of you, for accomplishing one of your goals you have so long desired. Which brings to mind the Scripture in Psalms 37:4 – Delight thyself also in the Lord: and He shall give thee the desires of thine heart.

Remember when things seem out of reach, Philippians 4:13 – I can do all things through Christ which strentheneth me. Sis. love you and may God continue to richly bless you in your endeavors.

Big Sis. and Co-laborer,
Missionary Yolonda Jolly

About the Author

Brenda, whose name mean **Enthusiastic**: fervent in spirit; serving the Lord; Romans (12:11).

Brenda Page was born, October 14th in Lubbock, Texas and was raised in Houston by her grandmother. She is pastored by Elder Freddie Hubbard and is a member of the Universal Church of God in Christ, where she is a licensed Evangelist Missionary and the Armor-bearer for her First Lady, Evangelist Debra Hubbard.

The biggest part of her ministry is encouraging the body of Christ and provoking them to walk in and fulfill their purpose. She believes without the Ministry of Helps functioning in the church, we are like ships at sea without a sail.

Her greatest desire is to please God, live holy, and let the Word dwell richly in her heart. Dining and studying God's Word has been her driving force and the love she has for the people of God.

ABOUT THE AUTHOR

Evangelist Missionary Page is the founder of the House of Page Ministries. The House of Page Ministries is dedicated to continual, effectual, fervant prayer, and intercession for families, leaders, the Body of Christ, and the community. Through the Annual House of Page Prayer Breakfast, the ministry has seen lives changed, answered prayers, and powerful testimonies from those who attend. Intercessors gather together for a morning of anointed and powerful prayer, praise, and worship.

Words from the Potter

The Lord gave the word: great was the Company of those published it.

> Psalms 68:11

According as he hath chosen us in him before the foundation of the world, that we should be holy and without blame before him in love.

> Ephesians 1:4

Faithful is he that calleth you, who also will do it.

> 1 Thessalonians 5:24

But ye are a chosen generation, a royal priesthood, a holy nation, a peculiar people; that ye should show forth the praises of him who hath called you out of darkness into his marvelous light.

> 1 Peter 2:9

And God hath set some in the church, first apostles, secondarily prophets, thirdly, teachers, after that miracles then the gifts of healings, helps, governments, diversities of tongues.

> 1 Corinthians 12:28

For if ye live after the flesh ye shall die: but if ye through the Spirit do mortify the deeds of the body, ye shall live. For as many as are led by the spirit of God, they are the sons of God.

> Romans 8:13-14

Wherefore the rather, brethren, give diligence to make your calling and election sure: for if ye do these things, ye shall never fall.

> 2 Peter 1:10

Now unto him that is able to keep you from falling, and to present you faultless before the presence of his glory with exceeding joy.

> Jude 1:24

Pleasing God is my goal, loving Him with my whole heart is my greatest desire. As the heart panteth after the water brooks, so panteth my soul after thee, O God.

> Psalm 42:1

In knowing the Word of God, the more you thirst you will read the Word. But when you become hungry not only will you read the Word, you will eat it also. In this process you can live the Word and walk in total victory.

Brethren be followers together of me, and mark them which walk so as ye have us for an example.

> Philippians 3:17

To order additional copies or for speaking
engagements, please contact:

Evangelist Missionary Brenda Page
c/o All That Productions, Inc.
P.O. Box 1594
Humble, Texas 77347-1594
(281) 878-2062

Notes

Notes

Notes

Notes

Notes

Notes

www.ingramcontent.com/pod-product-compliance
Lightning Source LLC
Chambersburg PA
CBHW060430050426
42449CB00009B/2218